T.J. ROHLEDER'S...
MIRACLE
METHOD

I0164007

The 3-Step Method to Change Your Life!

This book was written to help tens of millions of people end their emotional suffering. The simple 3-Step Method – you're about to discover – has created a real miracle in my life. That's why I call this process the Miracle Method and chose that name for this book. Now I am setting out to create a worldwide movement of others to help me teach this method to all of those who are suffering from depression, heartbreak, anxiety disorders, and addictions. Read my personal note on page 37. Then fill out the Form in back to find out more about this. — *T.J.*

This book – with its
life-changing message –
is presented to you by:

_____

T.J. Rohleder's Miracle Method
Copyright © MMXXI

ISBN: 1-933356-58-8

MM | MIRACLE METHOD INSTITUTE
www.MiracleMethod.net

Printed in the United States of America

SECTION ONE

You may not feel like it right now, but you can be happy, no matter what. This book will show you how. I'll lay out a simple 3-Step Method that can finally bring you the peace of mind you've been searching for. Maybe for the first time in your life! The principles behind the Miracle Method have helped millions of people and they can work for you. You can be happy and free from your emotional suffering, no matter what is happening or has happened to you in the past.

Using the Miracle Method will lead to...

- ✔ Increased happiness.
- ✔ **Better well-being.**
- ✔ Deeper satisfaction in all areas of your life.
- ✔ **A better relationship with God.**
- ✔ Lower stress and anxiety.
- ✔ **Overcoming thoughts of despair and feelings of hopelessness.**
- ✔ Elimination of <u>any</u> addiction or hang-up of <u>any</u> kind.
- ✔ **Confidence that comes from mastery over your negative emotions.**

All of This and More Can Be Yours by Using the 3-Step Miracle Method That Can Change Your Life.

The Miracle Method gives you a simple way

to get closer to God:

> The <u>first</u> step helps you **identify** the problem.

> The <u>second</u> step helps you **focus** on the solution.

> The <u>third</u> step helps you <u>turn it over to</u> **God**.

The first step helps you discover the beliefs that are creating your pain. Then, in the second step, you argue against those irrational thoughts and unreasonable demands. You identify the problem and create the solution. <u>Then you give it to God</u>. It's that simple. You uncover the source(s) of your emotional pain and replace those limiting ideas with fresh new thinking and a specific plan that is effective and spiritual.

This works! In time, this simple method will enable you to...

Master Your Negative Emotions and Make God the Center of Your Life.

It takes practice to get comfortable with the Miracle Method. Spend time each day going through this book. Stay with it for at least 30 days, you'll be amazed! The more you do it, the easier it will become. Within a few days, you'll begin to feel much happier, in spite of any problems you're going through. With **practice**, the Miracle Method really will produce a real miracle in your life!

I'll go over the 3 steps in a minute. Study them. Then begin to use the Miracle Method. Long-term miracles will come over a period of time, but you can begin to see **instant results** from the first time you use it!

THE KEY.

The **first step** in the Miracle Method helps you discover the problems with your current thinking that are causing your emotional pain. Once you do that, you simply use the **second step** to argue against that thinking, so you can replace your faulty thinking with empowering new thoughts and beliefs. The **third step** lets you turn it over to God and begin to develop an effective prayer life.

It's simple. And it works. Every time you feel angry, sad, worried, frustrated, lonely, depressed, or resentful, use the Miracle Method to challenge those thoughts.

Before we dive in any deeper, I want to assure you...

This is <u>Not</u> Just Another Version of "Positive Thinking."

The Miracle Method is much more effective than mere positive thinking. Proponents of positive thinking want you to believe that if you simply decide to change the way you think, you'll fix your problems. The Miracle Method isn't about covering up your emotions. Instead, you use this Method to face the truth about your emotions, change your thinking, and ultimately give it all to God.

By itself, thinking positive is like putting a Band-Aid on a bad cut. That doesn't work. Before a wound can heal – before you even stitch it up – you must get the dirt and germs out. Otherwise, infection will set in. Positive thinking alone covers up the way you really think and feel about something. It's no fix. It's just a short-term patch.

The Miracle Method takes the opposite approach. This incredible method doesn't cover up or temporarily mask your problems, it eliminates them!

The Miracle Method heals your wounds. <u>**Including God in the third step makes the process**</u>

<u>whole in ways that traditional (godless) self-help</u>
<u>never will</u>.

This process is simple to understand. But don't let the simplicity fool you. The Miracle Method involves challenging your oldest and most **deeply held beliefs** about how you think <u>other people,</u> <u>you yourself,</u> <u>and the world</u> *should* be. These beliefs are often unconscious and habitual, so it may take time to recognize them, challenge them, and ultimately replace them with new beliefs and a deeper relationship with God that will lead you toward the happiness you deserve.

The 3 Step Method.

Here is the 3-Step Miracle Method in a nutshell:

A.   Write down your answers to the simple questions in both steps.

B.   Create counter beliefs, affirmations, and prayers.

C.   Let it all go and give it to God.

This simple process will immediately make you feel better. With God's help, it will change your life. It really works! It's simple. But it works. Try it right now. Experience this for yourself. Grab a few sheets of paper or a personal journal.

Start by thinking of a person or a situation that is bothering you now or has bothered you in the past. Can you picture this person or thing? Good. Then follow these steps:

STEP ONE: Identify what is making you upset.

What is the situation that is causing you to be angry, depressed, resentful, frustrated, confused, unmotivated, etc.? Focus on these things for a minute before you continue.

Then pull out a pad of paper and ask yourself these questions...

A.   What is upsetting me?

This question lets you focus on the person or situation that is making you upset. Think of something that is bothering you now or was in the past. These events can be major: Job loss, serious illness, someone you can't seem to forgive, death of a loved one, or failing at something you care about. They can also be a series of minor annoyances that add-up over time, such as a boss, friend, or neighbor who treats you poorly, too many things on your schedule, heavy traffic, etc. **These activating events always have something to do with what you want to happen being interfered with**.

B. How does that make me feel?

This question puts you in touch with the **emotions** you are feeling (mad, sad, frustrated, hurt, lonely, overwhelmed, depressed, afraid, etc.) and your **behaviors** that are the result of the things that happen to you. For best results, answer these questions by writing as much as you can, as fast as you can. **Write fast and don't think too much about what you're writing!** Vent your feelings on paper. And remember: Nobody will see anything you write. This is between you and God.

C. What am I thinking that caused this feeling?

This question lets you examine your thoughts and attitudes about the first two questions. These thoughts can be RATIONAL (reality based, logical, and self helping) or IRRATIONAL (demanding and wishful thinking that's based on illogical and self-defeating thoughts). You can analyze all these thoughts later. For now, it's important to write down your answer to these questions as **fast** as you can.

Ask and answer those questions as fast as

you can. Then follow the next step...

STEP TWO: Replace your limiting thoughts with new beliefs, and then counterpunch!

Step two lets you challenge your limiting beliefs and then replace them with new beliefs that are the **opposite** of what you wrote down in step one. Answer the questions below, while also looking at what you already wrote in the previous step:

A. **How many ways can I <u>dispute</u> this?**

This question forces you to challenge the way you think. Use it to create new arguments against the answers you came up with while answering the questions in Step One. **When you do this, you argue against your irrational beliefs and unreasonable demands.** <u>Always write out your answers so you can see them on paper</u>. Then, when you have written all you can, go onto the final two questions in this step.

B. **What empowering <u>new</u> beliefs can I <u>replace</u> it with?**

There's no limit to the amount of <u>new and empowering thoughts</u> you can come up with. **Just write until you feel better.** Remember, you are doing this for yourself. <u>This is totally private</u>. Nobody but you and God will see your answers.

C.   Which answers do I feel the strongest about?

Complete this step by summarizing your favorite answers to the first two questions. Take your best answers and create as many counter affirmations or beliefs as you can. Choose the answers you feel the strongest about. Then write down a few brief affirmations or prayers. Re-read them throughout the day and follow the last step.

STEP THREE: Give It to God.

The Miracle Method helps you get closer to God. Take your best ideas from the prior step and turn them into a letter (a written-down prayer) to God. Then put your letter in your own special place that I call the "God Box." This can be a shoebox or any container. This is the most important step, so don't skip it. **Summarize the best answers you received during Step Two and put them in the form of a personal letter that you write directly to God.** Then say a prayer to God as you fold it up and drop it in your God Box. As you do this on a regular basis, it will help you develop a real and lasting relationship with God. You'll be refreshed as you work through your emotions and turning it all over to God's supernatural love and care.

Before we move on, I need to get this off my chest:

Self-help without God is <u>worthless</u>.

There was a time when I valued secular self-help. I used to live in a condo that was situated above a bookstore. I loved sitting at the bookstore browsing through all the self-help section. But <u>those days are over</u>. Today, I firmly believe that self-help without God has little value. Step Three is the strong spiritual component that can produce a real miracle in your life.

<u>The 'God Box' is a simple way to connect with God, to let Him help you deal with your emotional upsets. But it's also a helpful tool to use even when there's nothing upsetting you!</u> Because of this, the 'God Box' can be its own 'method-within-the-method' that will help you enjoy a better, more deeply personal connection with God. Even when you don't feel the need to use the first two steps in the Miracle Method, the 'God Box' can be used by itself to help you continue to develop a deeper relationship with God.

What does God really want for your life?

I have no idea! That's for you and God to figure out! **But what I can tell you is what God DOESN'T want for you.** <u>Here</u> <u>it</u> <u>is</u>: He doesn't want you to be angry, guilty, depressed, feeling bad about yourself, resentful, irritable, overwhelmed, upset, lustful, envious, filled with hatred and negativity, feeling shame, etc.

<u>Consider</u> <u>this</u>: What God does want for you is quite possibly the exact opposite of all of that. He wants you to feel excited about your life! He wants you to feel good about who you are and your rightful place in His world. He wants you to experience peace and love and confidence and a feeling of power over your life. He wants you to have more of the best that life has, so you're in a position to give more of what you have to as many other people as possible.

I BELIEVE GOD WANTS YOU TO BE STRONG!

A weak, defeated, depressed, dependent, angry, stressed-out, poverty-poor person has no power to give anything to anyone. God wants you to

13

be strong so you can lift others up! Think about it like this: 1,000 weak, dependent, lazy, depressed, unmotivated people will never produce even one powerful person. Even one million weak people could never produce one super-strong person. Strong people create more strong people. Only a strong person can ever offer any kind of strength and power to another person.

Doing things to become stronger is simple. It's not easy. But it is simple. Here is is: The more you feed the strong, positive side of you, the less power the negative aspects will have over you. Make the decision right now that your life is too short and precious to be angry, lonely, upset, angry, resentful, greedy, self-centered, egotistical, sad, depressed, etc. It's way too short. It's too sacred!

GET STARTED NOW

With all this said, it's easy to start using the Miracle Method... **This can be done with as few as three sheets of paper:**

Sheet 1: Write down the thoughts that are upsetting you.

Sheet 2: Write down the counter beliefs that are the **opposite** of sheet one.

Sheet 3: Write your personal note to God that summarizes what you wrote on the second sheet. Write it down and drop it in your God Box.

Start now: Follow the first step to identify your core problems. Then use the second step to dispute these thoughts in as many ways as possible. Turn to Section 2 and choose the empowering new thoughts and beliefs that you can immediately focus on. **I have used each one of these beliefs many times**. Each one has helped me in important ways. I know they can help you, too.

The 100 beliefs in Section Two are only the tips of the iceberg! These came from a list of thousands of beliefs I've personally used over the years. I want you to have all of them for your own Second Step. Now, you can get this complete list of 1,000s of additional beliefs and other great information about the Miracle Method that I didn't have room to give you in this small book.

More on this in a minute. For now, just choose the beliefs you like the most. Then write down your own list of empowering beliefs. Then use the final step to write a brief letter to God and turn it all over to Him. For best results, <u>always</u> do this on paper, while <u>always</u> writing as fast as you can.

TRY THE MIRACLE METHOD
NOW... IT WORKS!

The Miracle Method is simple to use, and it works! <u>All you do is quickly answer the questions in the first two steps and then turn it over to God</u>. This Method works because it lets you identify and challenge the thoughts that cause you to suffer, and then develop the habit of turning these things over to God.

The final two steps let you argue <u>against</u> the irrational beliefs or unreasonable demands that cause you to be upset and replace them with empowering new beliefs. After that, you use the third Step to let it go.

> <u>Understand this</u>: **The people and situations in your life do not have the power to make you happy or sad. It's what you say to yourself about these people and events that make you feel the way you do.**

<u>**You create your own emotions**</u>. The problems in your life, by themselves, don't make you worried or stressed out. You make yourself feel this way. This is good news, because it means that you have the power! Once you accept this and get good at using the Miracle Method, you can be happy in spite of whatever problems you're facing.

The Miracle Method will change your life because it makes you the master of your emotions and helps you to have a real and growing personal relationship with God.

The Miracle Method leads to emotional mastery. This will be your greatest skill because it gives you the power to be happy, no matter what life throws at you. The same problems that cause other people to break down will cause you to break records! **The first two steps in the Miracle Method give you a practical way to look at your situations differently.** Then, the third step gives you an effective way to deepen your personal relationship with God.

Use the Method over a period of time and miracles will occur.

The same problems that drive you crazy right now won't even phase you. You'll have the ability to be happy no matter what! This is not therapy, it's reeducation and practical spirituality. You're teaching yourself to think and feel differently, while learning how to let God play a bigger role in your life. You're challenging and changing your beliefs, and with enough practice, you will change the way you feel. This works when you work it. Make it a habit and it will change your life!

WHY IT WORKS

The MIRACLE METHOD works because:
1. It makes it easy to identify your limiting beliefs and unreasonable demands. **2.** Then you CHALLENGE THEM by creating a list of the reasons why these beliefs are false. **3.** Then you replace your original beliefs with new beliefs and positive prayers that energize and empower you to move forward.

This really can produce a miracle in your life. **But let me be 100% clear;**

The miracles that you can experience by using the Miracle Method come from you and God. It's how you use the 3 steps in this method that will produce the actual 'miracles' that will show up in your life.

The miracles come from God as He heals your mind and body. It's true that God does work through other people (including the person who made this book available to you!), but the real miracles that you can experience with this method will always come from your ability to allow God to help you. For best results, commit to using this 3-step method for at least one month. Like any spiritual program, the more you commit to it and the harder you work at it (and the more you lean into God), the better your results can be.

Later, I'll tell you more about this in the bigger book and how to get a copy.

For now, know this: **True confidence does not come from having things, it comes from handling things.** The Miracle Method gives you a simple way to do this. The more you use these steps, the better you'll get and the more power you'll have. In time, you will develop the total confidence that comes from knowing that, with God's help, you can handle whatever comes your way.

How I First Used the Miracle Method to Turn My Entire Life Around.

Some time ago, I was very upset over some terrible financial problems that I was going through. It got so bad, that all I could think about was killing myself. The pain was so great I didn't want to go on. **I was totally depressed.** I had lost all my savings. I was deeply in debt. And there seemed to be no way out, except to declare bankruptcy. The joke was that I didn't even have enough money to pay the fees to go bankrupt! How crazy is that!?!

I felt like a total failure. Like I had let so

many people down.

For years, my business brought in millions of dollars with little effort. We could do no wrong. Everything we touched seemed to turn to gold. But all of the sudden, my business was virtually bankrupt. I had brought in, spent, and lost a fortune. I felt deeply ashamed. I felt like a failure. In spite of my past success, all I could focus on was my short-term failures – and it was consuming me. I was drowning.

I became extremely depressed. I was a huge disappointment to myself and the people around me. I had convinced myself that my previous success was a fluke. I told myself that my best years were over. I was washed up. I was filled with all kinds of resentment and bad feelings towards myself and others. It got so bad, so fast...

I felt that my life was no longer worth living.

The emotional pain I felt was real. Every day was filled with new suffering. I thought that this misery was coming from the fact that my business and finances were in such terrible shape. **What I didn't realize at the time was that I was creating my suffering by the things I was telling myself about my situation.** For example, my belief was that these problems were impossible to solve. I believed they

were terrible, horrible, and absolutely devastating.
<u>Those</u> <u>deeply</u> <u>held</u> <u>beliefs</u> <u>were</u> <u>causing</u> <u>me</u> <u>to</u> <u>be</u>
<u>severely</u> <u>depressed</u>.

I became obsessed with thoughts like:

- "I **should** have done (_____)
  differently."

- "I **should** **not** have invested in
  (_____)."

- "I **should** have listened to
  (_____)."

- "I **must** **never** declare bankruptcy,
  because I will be a failure."

- "This is **impossible** to solve,
  because (_____)."

- "My best years are **over**, because
  (_____)."

- "I'd be **better** **off** **dead**, because
  (_____)."

- "There's **no** **way** I'll **ever** get out
  of this."

Those thoughts were driving me

crazy. I told myself I had let everyone down. I told myself I was a total failure. I told myself things were <u>never</u> going to get any better. Plus, I had terrible feelings of resentment for myself, other people, and even life itself. The more I thought these things, the more depressed and suicidal I became. It got so bad that I could barely get out of bed. Even the smallest decisions were extremely painful. Even when I was awake, I acted like a walking zombie.

Thank God I discovered the Miracle Method. *I know for a fact that...*

This Method Saved My Life.

My friend Jeff used this Method to cure his own depression, insanity, and suicidal tendencies. He saw me suffering. He knew I felt hopeless. So he told me about the Miracle Method. <u>He wrote the simple steps down for me, just as someone else had written them down for him</u>. Then he coached me for a few weeks. There was no book. He just talked me through the steps and helped me begin to use them every day. I know it sounds a bit cliché to say that it worked right away. BUT IT DID! Almost immediately, I began to feel relief from the pain I was in. Over time, this simple method cured me of the pain and suffering from my irrational thoughts and beliefs.

✔ I began to dispute the negative thoughts that were the cause my emotional pain.

✔ I kept a growing list of reasons why my beliefs were false.

✔ I began to see things from a much different perspective.

✔ Then, the final step gave me a personal relationship with God.

I've kept this 3-Step Miracle Method close to my heart ever since. These simple actions have produced such miracles in my life that I decided to make the Miracle Method available to other people who are suffering greatly. This Miracle Method is perfect for everyone who is searching for a practical way to cope with the problems of life and deepen their relationship with God.

Before we continue to Section Two of this tiny book, let me take a minute to tell you how to get my giant Miracle Method manual at no additional cost.

Here's My Special Offer to You.

Thank you for studying this book. This small book came from my original manual with the same title. I wanted you to have a smaller book – with enough information about the Miracle Method – so you could use it and **prove** it works. Please keep this book close by. Re-read it often. Then practice using the Miracle Method until it becomes a way of life.

My mission is to help millions of people end their suffering. And now I'm inviting you to help me reach more people. How? You can start by purchasing a few of these small Miracle Method books to give away to your friends, family, or anyone else you think could benefit. Fill out the Form you'll find at the back of this book. Order a box of 100 books, and I will give you a copy of the GIANT MIRACLE METHOD MANUAL at no extra cost. <u>It will be yours free</u>! This is a $49 value, yours at no extra cost. Along with my giant manual, I will also send you a package of information that shows you how you can become a Certified Miracle Method Instructor. I'm looking for Instructors to help me share the Miracle Method with churches and other civic organizations. It's a simple way to earn extra money while helping others learn this unique method to end their emotional suffering. Although there's no pressure, I feel like anyone who orders a box of 100 Miracle Method Books might be perfect to talk to about being an Instructor. Fill out the form at the end of this book and order today.

Thank you for reading this and God bless you. *Let's continue to Section Two...*

SECTION TWO

Empowering New Beliefs
to Change Your Life

The Miracle Method makes it easy to identify and then challenge your current thoughts and feelings. This section gives you 100 of my favorite beliefs that have empowered me as I work through the final steps. You will notice that they are written in the first person so that they can be easily applied as you build your new ways of thinking.

It's simple: Go through the first step to identify the problems that are causing your pain and then dispute them. Then do the second step. Open this section up and choose the new beliefs you like the most. Then write them down, turn them over to God in the form of a personal prayer.

Start with my beliefs as you work through the second step. Take the best ones that speak the loudest to you and make them your own. Then slowly create your own list of empowering new beliefs. Go over the first part of this book to remind yourself of how each step works. Then turn to this section and discover my favorite empowering new thoughts and beliefs that you can focus on as you work through the final steps.

With that in mind, here are 100 of my favorite beliefs that (WITH GOD!) helped me end my

own emotional suffering:

1.   Adversity is my teacher.

2.   EVERY STRESSFUL THOUGHT IS A LIE: 90% of the things in my life are right and about 10% are wrong. If I want to be happy, all I have to do is focus on the 90% that are right and ignore the 10% that are wrong. If I want to be stressed out, all I have to do is focus on the 10% that are wrong and ignore the 90% that are right.

3.   Whatever I pray an ask for, when I believe I have received it, it will be mine. (Mark 11:24).

4.   Starting today, I will stop looking at those things that are labeled as "hard" as being "bad." If I fill my life with things that I label as "easy" and "comfortable," I will never become all I am capable of being. It is only in challenging myself that I will feel totally alive, energized and engaged!

5.   I become who I associate with. So I am filling my days with people who are moving forward at the highest level and achieving the

things I want to achieve.

6.   I choose to believe that my best is
      yet to be.

7.   When I am going through really bad
      situations, always ask myself: "What's
      good about this?" I will immediately
      say, 'NOTHING!!!' So then I ask:
      "What could be good about this?" Or,
      if not 'good', then: "What's
      interesting?" OR: "What's funny?" I
      keep asking these questions until I get
      some solid answers. THE KEY: I can't
      control or change many of the
      situations I encounter in life, but I can
      change what these situations mean. I
      find and embrace the most
      empowering meanings.

8.   What I see depends mainly on what
      I look for. To one person the world
      is desolate, dull and empty – to
      another the same world looks rich,
      interesting and full of meaning. The
      choice is up to me. If I look at life
      the WRONG WAY there is always
      cause for alarm. I know that most
      people complain because roses
      have thorns. Instead I am thankful
      that thorns have roses.

9. I will make it through this, no matter what!

10. Turning things over to God makes me stronger.

11. I trust God more and worry less.

12. I live one day at a time.

13. It's better to bend than to break.

14. I find the positive meaning in my pain.

15. God always forgives me, so I forgive myself. I can't change the past, so I let it go and learn from it. My past mistakes are my greatest teachers. I know that good judgment comes from experience and experience comes from bad judgment.

16. My attitude is more important than any of the facts I am faced with.

17. With God on my side, I am stronger than I think.

18. I am who I decide to be. And I can change that, anytime I want.

19. God can't give it to me until I set it into motion.

20. I see myself with kind eyes.

21.   I forgive everyone and everything.

22.   All growth is 3 steps forward and 2 steps back.

23.   Nobody can make me feel inferior (or any other way) without my consent.

24.   Pain is inevitable. Suffering is optional.

25.   I forgive people for myself – and not for their benefit. I do it for my own sanity and peace of mind.

26.   Problems are good because they spur me into action, and life is action.

27.   I can do all things through Christ who gives me strength. (Philippians 4:13)

28.   Every day of my life is a do-over.

29.   I can never fully understand one thing without many other things to compare it with.

30.   Whenever I think I CAN or I CAN'T do something, I'm right.

31.   I am a co-creator with God.

32.   I practice getting excited!

33.   My life is definitely NOT worth living

without a strong relationship with God.

34. Trying to pray to God is praying.

35. What I think, feel and believe about myself is more important than others opinions.

36. I make the best of whatever happens.

37. I thank God that I am alive!

38. Getting really good at anything will <u>always</u> make me feel better about myself.

39. I take total responsibility for my own health and happiness.

40. I focus on what is most important in my life, and why.

41. Through the power of God in me, I am a great _____.

42. I have faith that better days are ahead.

43. I never take myself too seriously.

44. I let go of **<u>all</u>** of my resentments towards myself and others.

45. I know that God is love and he loves me!

46. I never let my past ruin my life today.

47. I let God fight my battles!

48. Prayer changes me from the inside out.

49. People do not determine my destiny, God does.

50. I know that most people are for themselves and not against me (Thank God!).

51. I never let anyone crush my dreams.

52. I do what makes me feel most alive!

53. If it wasn't this it would be something else.

54. God can only do to me what he can first do through me.

55. Where there is hope for the future, there's strength for today.

56. It is what it is. It is what I make it.

57. I always do whatever comes next! No matter how difficult it is! I still do it!

58. I would rather be happy than be right!

59. With God all things are possible. (Not some things, ALL things!)

60. I am an imperfect person who sometimes behaves imperfectly.

61. I take private pleasure in being me!

62. I go as far as I can see, and when I get there I can see even further.

63. I NEVER GIVE UP!

64. I let go of unhappy people or they'll drag me down with them.

65. IT'S OKAY IF OTHERS DON'T LIKE ME!

66. I believe it before I see it.

67. MY ULTIMATE POWER: To develop the strong belief that everything happens for a reason, and this reason is positive and serves me in some great way. When I do this, nothing can destroy me. Nothing can deter me. Nothing can stop me.

68. My unreasonable demands and irrational beliefs make me unhappy.

69. I do one thing each day that leads me closer to my ultimate goal.

70. I love you and I forgive you.

71. My positive beliefs create my reality.

72. I NEVER TAKE ANYTHING PERSONALLY.

73. I don't wish things were easier, I wish I were better.

74. I let go and let God.

75. My past was not better – only different.

76. God never gives me more than I can handle.

77. HARD WORK IS GOOD FOR MY SOUL.

78. My feelings aren't facts about my situation.

79. I win because I think I can.

80. I can't have a spiritual awakening until I am in a spiritual place.

81. I am responsible for what I do, no matter how I feel.

82. The harder I work, the luckier I get.

83. I use humor to <u>defuse</u> the negative situations in my life.

84. The challenges I face make my life more interesting.

85. Will doing more of (_____) give me more of what I really want?

If not, I stop doing it!

86. I must believe it before I can receive it.

87. I never expect something for nothing.

88. The best things in my life aren't things.

89. God did not take me this far to leave me now.

90. In the end, only God can heal me.

91. All things in my life are difficult before they become easy.

92. I surround myself with people who are smarter and better than I am.

93. I LEARN BY DOING.

94. I follow my bliss.

95. I stay too busy to be miserable.

96. I will _____... No matter what!

97. I refuse to attack myself.

98. God is bigger than all of my problems.

99. I am teaching myself how to trust God.

100. I thank God for the amazing people

in my life.

There you have it. These are some of my greatest beliefs that have helped me to end my own emotional suffering. I hope you can use them (in your own unique way) to end your own emotional suffering.

These 100 beliefs came from a list of thousands of different beliefs that I have used to end my own pain. I'd love to send you the complete list and much, much more. It's all yours when you get my GIANT MIRACLE METHOD MANUAL. Get it free with your purchase of a box of 100 copies of this book. Or you can order a copy by filling out the Form on the last page of this book.

As we start to wrap up, here are...

A few key points to consider:

✔   Replacing your current beliefs that you identified in Step One with new and more empowering beliefs is what the second Step is all about. You now have a list of my 100 favorite beliefs.

✔   I chose these beliefs from my huge list of 1,000's of empowering beliefs... If you like these 100, you'll love my complete collection!

✔   I've used these beliefs many times

as I worked through the second
step. They've helped me greatly. I
know the right combination of them
can help you, too.

✔   I wanted you to only have the best
of my beliefs for now. However, if
you like these, then you will love my
complete list. *Best of all...*

My Huge Collection
Can Be Yours Free!

My GIANT MIRACLE METHOD MANUAL can be
yours free. Here's how: Just order 100 or more of these
small Miracle Method books to pass out to your friends
and family. Do this and I'll send you a copy of my GIANT
MANUAL for free! Or purchase a copy for $49.

The Miracle Method can change your life. It's
time to get started. Go back through this small book
and start with Step One. Use this Miracle Method on a
regular basis. In time, you will begin to feel less
emotional pain and begin to develop a deeper
relationship with God. You will begin to see and feel
real miracles overtaking your life.

SECTION THREE

My GIANT Miracle Method Manual Can Now Be Yours FREE!

I hope you've enjoyed this little book. This is an excerpt from my GIANT Manual. This larger Manual goes into much more depth about all 3 steps. It also contains hundreds of pages of empowering new beliefs and worksheets you can use to make the 3-step method part of your daily life. But that's not all! Send for my GIANT Manual, and I'll also send you several Vouchers that invite you to attend our ongoing Zoom Meetings, where I teach the Miracle Method and go over more resources from the GIANT Manual. Fill out the Form on the last page of this book. You can purchase a copy of my GIANT Manual for just $49. Or I'll send you a copy of my GIANT Manual FREE when you purchase 100 copies of this little book to hand out to friends, family, and people you care about.

This little book was written to give you a complete summary of the Miracle Method. Keep this little book with you all the time. Practice all 3 steps. But the true benefits come from MASTERING the Miracle Method. And you're going to want my GIANT Manual to help you master this method. Here's some of the benefits you'll experience by getting my GIANT Manual and making a deeper commitment to mastering the Miracle Method.

✔ You will find yourself becoming <u>less</u> upset or angry than ever before.

✔ <u>The things that are bothering you right now will stop bothering you</u>.

✔ You will see your problems in a whole new and empowering way.

✔ **You will feel closer to God than <u>ever</u> before.**

✔ You'll love and accept yourself in a deeper way than you've ever experienced before.

✔ The things that are making you angry right now will have no power over you.

✔ **You'll find yourself laughing at the things that used to make you so upset.**

✔ You'll find yourself feeling good, even if nothing has changed.

✔ <u>You'll find yourself appreciating your life in a much deeper way</u>.

✔ You'll feel so good because you will finally have an effective prayer life.

✔ Your whole world will look different! It will seem miraculous because it is!

✔ You will have the power to deal with the hardest times.

✔ **You will love yourself fully and unconditionally.** You'll be able to look in the mirror and say "I love myself" – and really mean it.

✔ **You'll be amazed at the changes you see in yourself... And it won't take long!**

✔ You'll relax, maybe for the first time in years. You'll be at ease with the world in a way you've never experienced before the Miracle Method.

✔ You'll find new solutions to the problems that you are faced with right now.

✔ **You'll see the world through new eyes.** This alone will make you feel better about yourself (and your rightful place on the world) than you have ever felt.

✔ **You'll appreciate life at a very deep level.** You'll find yourself enjoying the little things, the way a young child does.

Master the Miracle Method and people will see a huge change in you. They'll say things like: "What's different about you?" Your life-change will make them curious!

You'll feel strong and victorious because you'll be the master of your emotions. You'll see other people getting upset about things that used to make you upset, and you'll know for a <u>fact</u> that the changes inside you are real.

Get Your GIANT Miracle Method Manual Right Now!

Fill out the Form at the end of this little book and get my GIANT Miracle Method Manual for just $49. Or it can be YOURS FREE with your purchase of 100 copies of this little book to share with friends, family, and anyone else you think will benefit from the Miracle Method.

An Invitation for You

Dear Reader,

I hope this book helps you greatly. The Miracle Method saved my life, and it has the power to help you and millions of other people. Do you know someone who is suffering right now? Maybe they're dealing with an extremely painful bout of depression, like I was. Perhaps they have issues with anger or addiction? Or they just need to feel better about themselves and gain more confidence to handle the challenges that life brings to all of us.

If so, please use the form that follows this to order a quantity of these Miracle Method books. This is an easy way you can help me spread the news about this powerful and proven method and help end the emotional suffering that your friends and loved ones may be going through.

Please Join Me

I am on a mission to share the Miracle Method with the tens of millions of people around the world who are suffering like I did for so many years. If you find the Miracle Method helpful and have enjoyed reading this book, you may be interested in becoming one of my Miracle Method Certified Instructors. As an Instructor, you will work directly with me and my team, to help us get the message out about the Miracle Method. With this position, you can experience the joy of helping other people and even earn a comfortable living doing it.

So please use the form on the next page to order more of these books. Or you can visit MiracleMethod.net to place your order. By purchasing a box of 100 copies, you'll also receive my GIANT MANUAL at no extra cost. Along with your order, I will also include complete information about how you can become a Miracle Method Certified Instructor.

Sincerely,

T.J. Rohleder

The Miracle Method Will Change Your Life Because It Makes You the Master of Your Emotions and Helps You to Have a Real and Growing Personal Relationship with God.

www.ingramcontent.com/pod-product-compliance
Lightning Source LLC
Chambersburg PA
CBHW020442030426
42337CB00014B/1348